Daydream

Pattern Collection

12 Crochet &
Knit Projects

LEISURE ARTS, INC. • Maumelle, Arkansas

CONTENTS

Astrakhan Loop Crochet Pillow

EASY

MEASUREMENT
Approx 20" [51 cm] square

GAUGE
7 sc and 8 rows = 4" [10 cm]

MATERIALS

SUPER BULKY 6

Bernat® Blanket™
(10.5 oz/300 g; 220 yds/201 m)

☐ Dark Gray (10044) - 5 balls **or** 1040 yds/947 m

☐ Size U.S. L/11 (8 mm) crochet hook **or size needed to obtain gauge**

☐ Stitch marker

☐ 20" [51 cm] square pillow form

☐ 18" [45.5 cm] zipper (optional)

☐ Sewing thread and needle (optional if applying zipper)

INSTRUCTIONS

PILLOW

Note: Pillow is worked in one piece from top edge down.

Ch 34.

1st rnd: 1 Sc in 2nd ch from hook. 1 sc in each ch to last ch. 3 sc in last ch. Working into opposite side of ch, 1 sc in each of next 32 ch. 2 sc in last ch. Join with sl st to first sc. 70 sc. Place marker on last st and move this marker up each rnd.

2nd rnd: *Ch 6. Sl st in front loop only of next sc. Rep from * around. Join with sl st to front loop only of first sc.

3rd rnd: Holding ch-6 loops forward to reveal rem back loop of each sc in previous rnd, ch 1. 1 sc in rem back loop of first sc. *1 sc in rem back loop of next sc. Rep from * around. Join with sl st to first sc.

Rep last 2 rnds for Chain Loop Pat until work from beg measures 20" [51 cm], ending on a 2nd rnd.

Fasten off.

FINISHING

Optional zipper application:

- Sew 1" [2.5 cm] seam at each end, leaving 18" [45.5 cm] opening.
- Pin zipper in position and sew into opening using needle and thread.

Sew entire lower edge closed if you are not applying zipper.

Big Knit Bolster

●○○○ **BASIC**

MEASUREMENTS

Approx 6" [15 cm] x 17 (22)" [43 (56) cm] long

GAUGE

5.5 sts and 9 rows = 4" [10 cm] in garter st

MATERIALS

Bernat® Blanket Extra™ (10.5 oz/300 g; 97 yds/87 m)

Pillow Length: 17" (22")

- ☐ Vapor Gray (27002) - 2 (3) balls
- ☐ Size U.S. 15 (10 mm) knitting needles **or size needed to obtain gauge**
- ☐ Bolster pillow form 7" [18 cm] x 17 (22)" [43 (56) cm] long
- ☐ 5 yds/4.7 m of worsted weight yarn in matching shade

INSTRUCTIONS

Cast on 30 (36) stitches (sts) loosely.

1st and 2nd rows: Slip next st purlwise (Sl1P). Knit to last st. Turn. Leave remaining (rem) st unworked.

3rd and 4th rows: Sl1P. Knit to end of row.

Repeat (Rep) last 2 rows of garter st until work from beg measures approx 20" [51 cm] **or** length to fit around bolster form.

Bind off.

Insert bolster form. Sew side seam.

Thread worsted weight yarn through side sts. Pull tightly. Fasten securely.

Rep for opposite side.

Tassels (make 2): Wrap yarn around 6" [15 cm] piece of cardboard 15 times.

Tie securely at one end. Cut across opposite end.

Wrap yarn 4 times around tassel 1½" [4 cm] from tied end and fasten securely.

Attach 1 Tassel to each end.

Bobble & Fringe Blanket

EASY

MEASUREMENTS
Approx 55" x 59" [139.5 cm x 150 cm] excluding fringe

GAUGE
7 dc and 4 rows = 4" [10 cm]

MATERIALS

Bernat® Softee® Chunky™ SUPER BULKY 6

(14 oz/400 g; 431 yds/394 m)

- ☐ Faded Denim (30114) - 5 balls
- ☐ Size U.S. L/11 (8 mm) crochet hook **or size needed to obtain gauge**

STITCH GUIDE

DOUBLE CROCHET 3/5 TOGETHER *(abbreviated Dc3/5tog)*

(Yoh and draw up a loop in indicated space. Yoh and draw through 2 loops on hook) 3(5) times. Yoh and draw through all loops on hook.

POPCORN

Work 5 dc into indicated space. Drop loop from hook. Insert hook from front to back into first dc of 5 dc group. Pull dropped loop through stitch.

INSTRUCTIONS

BLANKET

Note: Ch 3 at beg of rows counts as dc throughout.

Ch 125 (multiple of 24 ch + 29).
See diagram on page 11.

1st row: (RS). Skip first 3 ch. Dc3tog over next 3 ch (counts as 2 dc). 1 dc in each of next 9 ch. 5 dc in next ch. 1 dc in each of next 9 ch. *Dc5tog over next 5 ch. 1 dc in each of next 9 ch. 5 dc in next ch. 1 dc in each of next 9 ch. Rep from * to last 4 ch. Dc3tog over next 3 ch. 1 dc in last ch. Turn.

2nd row: Ch 3 (counts as dc here and throughout). Dc3tog. 1 dc in each of next 9 dc. 5 dc in next dc. 1 dc in each of next 9 dc. *Dc5tog. 1 dc in each of next 9 dc. 5 dc in next dc. 1 dc in each of next 9 dc. Rep from * to last 4 sts. Dc3tog. 1 dc in last dc. Turn.

3rd row: Ch 3. Dc3tog. (Ch 1. Skip next dc. 1 dc in next dc) 4 times. Ch 1. Skip next dc. 5 dc in next dc. (Ch 1. Skip next dc. 1 dc in next dc) 4 times. *Ch 1. Skip next dc. Dc5tog. (Ch 1. Skip next dc. 1 dc in next dc) 4 times. Ch 1. Skip next dc. 5 dc in next dc. (Ch 1. Skip next dc. 1 dc in next dc) 4 times. Rep from * to last 5 sts. Ch 1. Skip next dc. Dc3tog. 1 dc in last dc. Turn.

4th row: Ch 3. Dc3tog. 1 dc in next ch-1 sp. (1 dc in next dc. 1 dc in next ch-1 sp) 3 times. 1 dc in each of next 2 dc. 5 dc in next dc. 1 dc in each of next 2 dc. 1 dc in next ch-1 sp. (1 dc in next dc. 1 dc in next ch-1 sp) 3 times. *Dc5tog. 1 dc in next ch-1 sp. (1 dc in next dc. 1 dc in next ch-1 sp) 3 times. 1 dc in each of next 2 dc. 5 dc in next dc. 1 dc in each of next 2 dc. 1 dc in next ch-1 sp. (1 dc in next dc. 1 dc in next ch-1 sp) 3 times. Rep from * to last 4 sts. Dc3tog. 1 dc in last dc. Turn.

5th row: Ch 3. Dc3tog. (Ch 2. Skip next dc. Popcorn in next dc) 4 times. Ch 2. Skip next dc. (Popcorn, Ch 3, Popcorn) in next dc. (Ch 2. Skip next dc. Popcorn in next dc) 4 times. *Ch 2. Skip next dc. Dc5tog. (Ch 2. Skip next dc. Popcorn in next dc) 4 times. Ch 2. Skip next dc. (Popcorn. Ch 3. Popcorn) in next dc. (Ch 2. Skip next dc. Popcorn in next dc) 4 times. Rep from * to last 5 sts. Ch 2. Skip next dc. Dc3tog. 1 dc in last dc. Turn.

6th row: Ch 3. 2 dc in each of next 5 ch-2 sps. 5 dc in next ch-3 sp. *2 dc in each of next 4 ch-2 sps. 1 dc in next ch-2 sp. 1 dc in next dc. 1 dc in next ch-2 sp. 2 dc in each of next 4 ch-2 sps. 5 dc in next ch-3 sp. Rep from * to last 5 ch-2 sps. 2 dc in each of last 5 ch-2 sps. Skip next dc. 1 dc in last dc. Turn.

7th to 10th rows: As 2nd row.

11th row: Working in back loops only, as 3rd row.

Rep 4th to 11th rows until work from beg measures approx 59" [150 cm], ending on a 4th row.

Next row: As 2nd row.

Fasten off.

Fringe: Cut lengths of yarn 12" [30.5 cm]. Taking 2 strands tog, knot into fringe along top and bottom edge of Blanket and into rem front loops of each 11th row repeated throughout Blanket.

Trim fringe evenly.

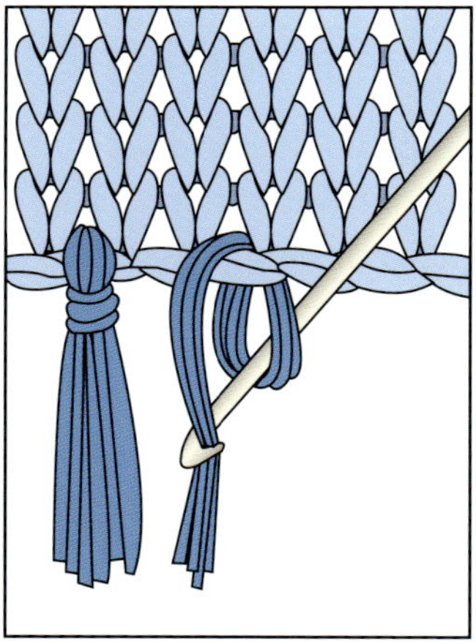

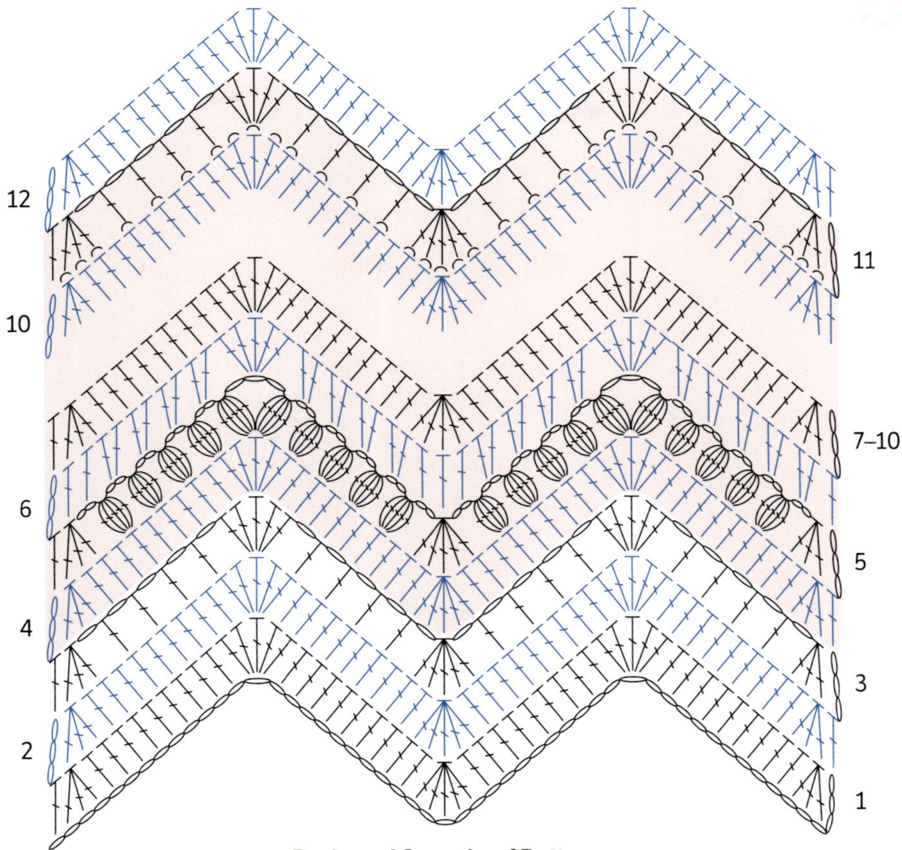

Reduced Sample of Pattern

KEY

- = chain (ch)
- = double crochet (dc)
- = double crochet 3 together (dc3tog)
- = double crochet 5 together (dc5tog)
- = popcorn
- = worked in back loop only
- = Repeat rows 4 to 11 for Pattern.

Cozy Toesies Crochet Rug

BASIC

MEASUREMENTS
Approx 32" [81.5 cm] wide x 50" [127 cm] long

GAUGE
6.5 sts and 6 rows = 4" [10 cm] in pat

MATERIALS

Bernat® Maker Big™ (JUMBO 7)
(8.8 oz/250 g; 77 yds/70 m)

- ☐ Smoke (25003) - 8 balls
- ☐ Size U.S. P/Q (15 mm) crochet hook **or size needed to obtain gauge**

INSTRUCTIONS

Chain (Ch) 52.

1st row: (Right side - RS). 1 Single crochet (sc) in 2nd ch from hook. *Ch 1. Skip next ch. 1 sc in next ch. Repeat (Rep) from * to end of chain. Turn. 51 stitches (sts).

2nd row: Ch 1. 1 sc in first sc. *1 sc in next ch-1 space (sp). Ch 1. Skip next sc. Rep from * to last 2 sts. 1 sc in next ch-1 sp. 1 sc in last sc. Turn.

3rd row: Ch 1. 1 sc in first sc. *Ch 1. Skip next sc. 1 sc in next ch-1 sp. Rep from * to last 2 sc. Ch 1. Skip next sc. 1 sc in last sc. Turn.

Rep last 2 rows for pattern (pat) until piece measures approx 50" [127 cm] long.

Finish off.

Fringe It Crochet Basket

EASY

MEASUREMENTS

Approx 16" [40.5 cm] wide x 18½" [47 cm] tall

GAUGE

7.5 sc and 8 rows = 4" [10 cm] with Bernat® Maker Big™

MATERIALS

Bernat® Maker Big™ JUMBO 7
(8.8 oz/250 g; 77 yds/70 m)

☐ Main Color (MC) Ivory (25002) - 7 balls

Caron® x Pantone™ SUPER BULKY 5
(3.5 oz/100 g; 127 yds/116 m)

☐ Ocean Surf (01008) - 2 braids

☐ Size U.S. N/15 (10 mm) crochet hook **or size needed to obtain gauge**

☐ Stitch markers

INSTRUCTIONS

BASKET

Note: Ch 2 at beg of row counts as hdc.

With MC ch 3.

1st rnd: (RS). 10 Hdc in 3rd ch from hook. Join with sl st to first hdc. 10 hdc.

2nd rnd: Ch 2. 2 hdc in each hdc around. Join with sl st to first hdc. 20 hdc.

3rd rnd: Ch 2. 1 hdc in first hdc. *2 hdc in next hdc. 1 hdc in next hdc. Rep from * to last hdc. 2 hdc in last hdc. Join with sl st to first hdc. 30 hdc.

4th rnd: Ch 2. 1 hdc in each of first 2 hdc. *2 hdc in next hdc. 1 hdc in each of next 2 hdc. Rep from * to last hdc. 2 hdc in last hdc. Join with sl st to first hdc. 40 hdc.

5th rnd: Ch 2. 1 hdc in each of first 3 hdc. *2 hdc in next hdc. 1 hdc in each of next 3 hdc. Rep from * to last hdc. 2 hdc in last hdc. Join with sl st to first hdc. 50 hdc.

6th rnd: Ch 2. 1 hdc in each of first 4 hdc. *2 hdc in next hdc. 1 hdc in each of next 4 hdc. Rep from * to last hdc. 2 hdc in last hdc. Join with sl st to first hdc. 60 hdc.

7th rnd: Ch 2. 1 hdc in each of first 5 hdc. *2 hdc in next hdc. 1 hdc in each of next 5 hdc. Rep from * to last hdc. 2 hdc in last hdc. Join with sl st to first hdc. 70 hdc.

8th rnd: Ch 2. 1 hdc in each of first 6 hdc. *2 hdc in next hdc. 1 hdc in each of next 6 hdc. Rep from * to last hdc. 2 hdc in last hdc. Join with sl st to first hdc. 80 hdc.

9th rnd: Ch 2. 1 hdc in each of first 7 hdc. *2 hdc in next hdc. 1 hdc in each of next 7 hdc. Rep from * to last hdc. 2 hdc in last hdc. Join with sl st to first hdc. 90 hdc.

10th rnd: Ch 2. 1 hdc in each of first 8 hdc. *2 hdc in next hdc. 1 hdc in each of next 8 hdc. Rep from * to last hdc. 2 hdc in last hdc. Join with sl st to first hdc. 100 hdc.

11th rnd: Ch 1. Working in back loops only, 1 sc in each hdc around. Join with sl st to first sc.

12th rnd: Ch 1. 1 sc in each sc around. Join with sl st to first sc.

Rep 12th rnd until work from 11th rnd measures 12" [30.5 cm].

Next 6 rnds: Ch 1. 1 sc in each sc around. Join with sl st to first sc. Turn. Place marker at end of each rnd and turn work at end of each rnd.

Next rnd: (RS). Ch 1. 1 sc in each sc around. Join with sl st to first sc. Do **not** turn.

Rep last rnd until work from 11th rnd measures 18" [45.5 cm].

Next rnd: Ch 1. Working from **left** to **right** instead of from right to left as usual, work 1 reverse sc in each sc around. Join with sl st to first sc.

Fasten off.

FINISHING

Fringe: Cut strands of A, B, C, D, and E 14" [35.5 cm] long.

A: 19-4026	**D:** 13-0000
B: 19-4044	**E:** 11-4001
C: 16-0000	

*Taking 2 strands of A, knot fringe into front bar of first 5 sts of 2nd marked rnd. Skip next 5 sts. Rep from * around.

Trim Fringe as shown in picture.

*Taking 2 strands of E, knot fringe into front bar of first 5 sts of 4th marked rnd. Taking 2 strands of C, knot fringe into front bar of next 5 sts. Rep from * around.

Trim Fringe as shown in picture.

*Taking 2 strands of D, knot fringe in front bar of first 5 sts of 6th marked rnd. Taking 2 strands of B, knot fringe in front bar of next 5 sts. Rep from * around.

Trim Fringe as shown in picture.

Knit Graphic Headboard

●●○○ EASY

HEADBOARD SIZES

Full: 56" x 48" [142 cm x 122 cm]
Queen: 62" x 48" [157.5 cm x 122 cm]
King: 80" x 48" [203 cm x 122 cm]

GAUGE

6 sts and 8 rows = 4" [10 cm]

MATERIALS

Bernat® Maker Big™ JUMBO 7

(8.8 oz/250 g; 77 yds/70 m)

- ☐ Ivory (25002)
  - **FULL:** 9 balls
  - **QUEEN:** 12 balls
  - **KING:** 16 balls
- ☐ Size U.S. 17 (12.75 mm) circular knitting needles 40" [101.5 cm] long **or size needed to obtain gauge**
- ☐ Plywood or oriented strand board cut to measurements above
- ☐ Quilt batting to cover headboard measurements plus 4" [10 cm] wrap-over allowance
- ☐ Staple gun and staples
- ☐ Spray glue

INSTRUCTIONS

The instructions are written for smallest size. If changes are necessary for larger size(s) the instructions will be written thus ( ). Numbers for each size are shown in the same color throughout the pattern. When only one number is given in black, it applies to all sizes.

Note: Accurate stitch and row gauge is very important to achieve finished measurements.

Cast on 88 (97-124) sts. Do **not** join. Working back and forth across needle in rows, proceed as follows:

(See Chart on page 21).

1st and 2nd rows: Knit.

3rd row: (RS). K2 (11-38). P 17. K 32. P 35. K2.

4th row: P2. K 35. P 32. K 17. P2 (11-38).

5th row: As 3rd row.

6th to 23rd rows: Rep 4th and 5th rows 9 times **more**.

24th row: P2. K 35. Purl to end of row.

25th row: K2 (11-38). P 49. K 37.

26th row: P 25. K 12. P 12. K 37. P2 (11-38).

27th row: K2 (11-38). P 37. K 12. P 12. K 25.

28th to 39th rows: Rep 26th and 27th rows 6 times **more**.

40th row: P 25. Knit to end of row.

41st row: K0 (0-11). P0 (0-18). K 51 (60-58). P 12. K 25.

42nd row: P 25. K 12. P 22. K 11. P 18 (27-25). K0 (0-18). P0 (0-11).

43rd row: K0 (0-11). P0 (0-18). K 18 (27-25). P 11. K 22. P 12. K 25.

44th to 53rd rows: Rep 42nd and 43rd rows 5 times **more**.

54th row: P2. K 68. P 18 (27-25). K0 (0-18). P0 (0-11).

55th row: K0 (0-11). P0 (0-18). K 18 (27-25). P1. K 10. P 22. K 20. P 15. K2.

56th row: P2. K 15. P 20. K 22. P 10. K1. P 18 (27-25). K0 (0-18). P0 (0-11).

57th row: As 55th row.

58th to 65th rows: Rep 56th and 57th rows 4 times **more**.

66th row: P2. K 15. P 20. K 22. P 10. K1. P 18 (27-25). K0 (0-29).

67th row: K0 (0-28). P0 (0-1). K 18 (27-25). P1. K 10. P 22. K 20. P 15. K2.

68th row: P2. K 15. P 20. K 22. P 10. K1. P 18 (27-25). K0 (0-1). P0 (0-28).

69th row: As 67th row.

70th and 71st rows: As 68th and 69th rows.

72nd row: P2. K 57. P 10. K1. P 18 (27-25). K0 (0-1). P0 (0-28).

73rd row: As 67th row.

74th and 75th rows: As 68th and 69th rows 6 times **more**.

76th row: P2. K 15. P 20. K 49 (58-59). P2 (2-28).

77th row: K2 (2-28). P 17 (26-27). K 10. P 22. K 20. P 15. K2.

78th row: P2. K 15. P 20. K 22. P 10. K 17 (26-27). P2 (2-28).

79th to 84th rows: As 77th and 78th rows 3 times **more**.

85th row: K2 (2-28). P 17 (26-27). K 10. (P1. K 20) twice. P 15. K2.

86th row: P2. K 15. (P 20. K1) twice. P 10. K 17 (26-27). P2 (2-28).

87th to 98th rows: As 85th and 86th rows 6 times **more**.

99th and 100th rows: Purl.

Bind off.

FINISHING

Apply glue to front of board.

Cover board in quilt batting, securing with staples at back.

Wrap board with knitted piece, noting 2 row selvage allowance at back and 2 row stitch selvage at either side, taking care to keep texture pat on knitted piece straight. Secure with staples at back.

Attach to wall or bed frame.

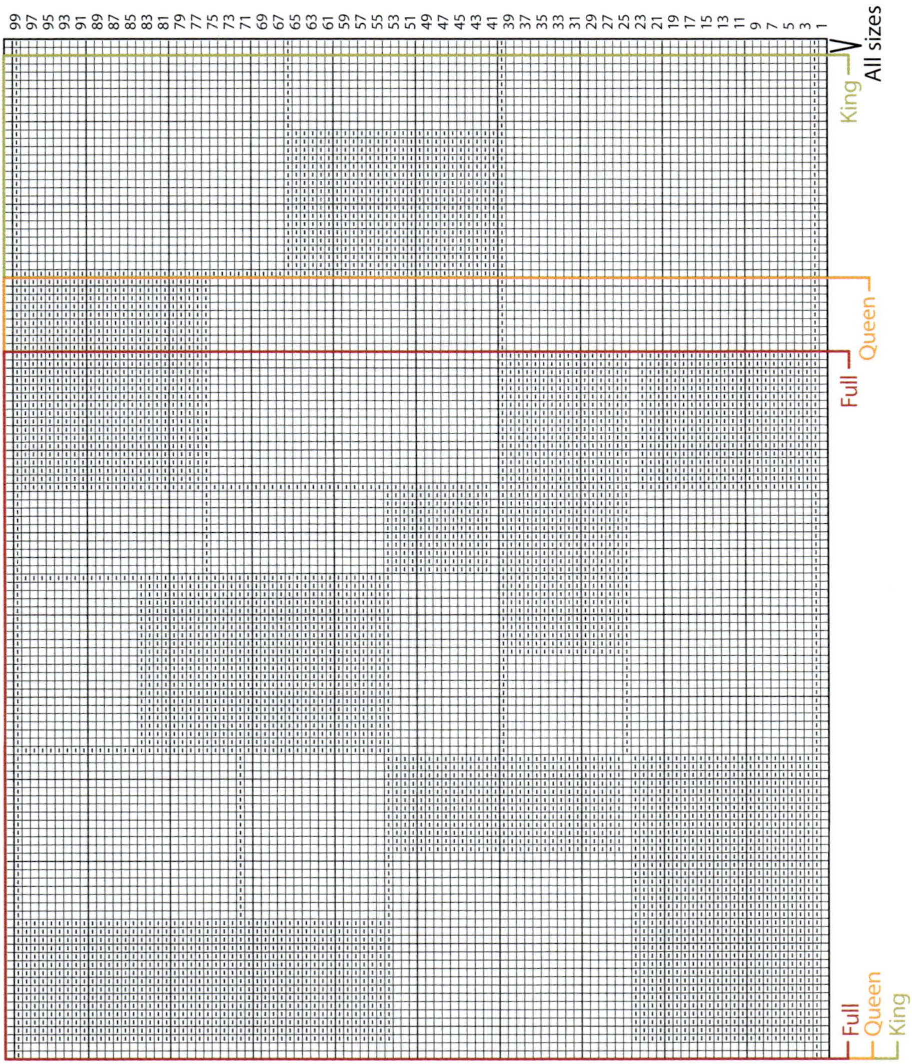

KEY

☐ = Knit on RS rows. Purl on WS rows.

▭ with – = Knit on WS rows. Purl on RS rows.

Loopy Corner Crochet Pillow

INTERMEDIATE

MEASUREMENT
Approx 20" [51 cm] square

GAUGE
7 sc and 8 rows = 4" [10 cm] with Bernat® Blanket™

MATERIALS

Bernat® Blanket™ (SUPER BULKY 6)
(10.5 oz/300 g; 220 yds/201 m)

☐ Main Color (MC)
Dark Gray (10044) **or**
Vintage White (10006) -
2 balls **or** 400 yds/364 m

Bernat® Alize Blanket EZ™ (BULKY 7)
(6.4 oz/180 g; 18 yds/16 m)

☐ Contrast A Dark Gray (37014) **or** Cream (37013) - 1 ball

☐ Size U.S. L/11 (8 mm) crochet hook **or size needed to obtain gauge**

☐ 20" [51 cm] square pillow form

☐ 1" [2.5 cm] button

STITCH GUIDE

SINGLE CROCHET 2/3 TOGETHER *(abbreviated Sc2/3tog)*

Draw up a loop in each of next 2/3 stitches. Yoh and draw through all loops on hook.

INSTRUCTIONS

FRONT

Notes:

- Loop section of Pillow is worked using MC for background sc rows while holding EZ yarn (A) in front of MC yarn and working each sc with MC **around** each space between loops of EZ yarn (A).
- Stitches are never worked *with* or *into* A yarn.
- Gently tug EZ yarn (A) loops to RS of work.

- EZ yarn (A) is held towards front of work (RS) **at all times** and always **below** MC. Pillow Front is worked diagonally, from corner to corner.

With MC, ch 2.

1st row: (WS). 2 Sc in 2nd ch from hook. Join A (leaving 3 loops of A yarn at side edge to weave in later).

2nd row: Holding A yarn in front of work (towards RS) with MC above, ch 1 with MC. With MC, [(catching A yarn between 2 loops) 2 sc in next sc] twice. 4 sc. Turn.

3rd row: Holding A yarn in back of work (towards RS) with MC above, ch 1 with MC. With MC, (catching A yarn between 2 loops for each sc across), 2 sc in first sc. 1 sc in each of next 2 sc. 2 sc in last sc. 6 sc. Turn.

4th row: Holding A yarn in front of work (towards RS) with MC above, ch 1 with MC. With MC, (catching A yarn between 2 loops for each sc across), 2 sc in first sc. 1 sc in each of next 4 sc. 2 sc in last sc. 8 sc. Turn.

5th row: Holding A yarn in back of work (towards RS) with MC above, ch 1 with MC. With MC, (catching A yarn between 2 loops for each sc across), 2 sc in first sc. 1 sc in each sc to last sc. 2 sc in last sc. 10 sc. Turn.

6th row: Holding A yarn in front of work (towards RS) with MC above, ch 1 with MC. With MC, (catching A yarn between 2 loops for each sc across), 2 sc in first sc. 1 sc in each sc to last sc. 2 sc in last sc. 12 sc. Turn.

7th row: As 5th row. 14 sc.

8th row: Holding A yarn in front of work (towards RS) with MC above, ch 1 with MC. With MC, (catching A yarn between 2 loops for each sc across), 1 sc in each sc to end of row. Turn.

9th to 28th rows: Rep 5th to 8th rows (working every 4th row without increases) 5 times **more**. 44 sts. Break A.

Cont with MC only for smooth section.

29th row: (WS). Ch 1. 1 sc in each of first 8 sc. (2 sc in next sc. 1 sc in each of next 8 sc) 4 times. Turn. 48 sc.

Next 4 rows: Ch 1. Sctog. 1 sc in each sc to last 2 sts. Sc2tog. Turn.

Next row: Ch 1. 1 sc in each st to end of row. Turn.

Rep last 5 rows 4 times **more**. 8 sts rem.

Next 2 rows: Ch 1. Sctog. 1 sc in each sc to last 2 sts. Sc2tog. Turn. 4 sts rem at end of 56th row.

Next row: Ch 1. (Sc2tog) twice.

Next row: Sc2tog. Finish off.

BACK

Pillow Back is worked in 2 pieces, with center back opening to insert pillow form.

With B, ch 37.

1st row: (RS). With B, 1 sc in 2nd ch from hook. 1 sc in each ch to end of chain. Turn. 36 sc.

2nd row: Ch 1. 1 sc in each sc to end of row. Turn.

Rep last row until work from beg measures 13" [33 cm].

Finish off.

Place markers on side edges 3" [7.5 cm] down from final row.

FINISHING

Overlap Back pieces at markers.

Sew overlapped sections of Back pieces tog at sides. Open section across center Back is to insert pillow form.

Sew side edges of Front and Back pieces tog. Using open sp between sts as buttonhole, sew button to center back.

Loopy Dots Crochet Blanket

EASY

MEASUREMENTS

Approx 54" x 60" [137 cm x 152.5 cm]

GAUGE

Blanket: 8 sts and 6 rows = 4" [10 cm] in pat with Bernat® Blanket™ and larger hook

Loopy Dots: 10 sc and 11 rows = 4" [10 cm] with Bernat® Velvet™ and smaller hook

MATERIALS

Bernat® Blanket™ SUPER BULKY 6

(10.5 oz/300 g; 220 yds/201 m)

- ☐ Main Color (MC) Vintage White (10006) - 6 balls **or** 1234 yds/1129 m

Bernat® Velvet™ BULKY 5

(10.5 oz/300 g; 315 yds/288 m)

- ☐ Contrast A Vapor Gray (32001) - 1 ball
- ☐ Contrast B Quiet Pink (32013) - 1 ball
- ☐ Contrast C Smokey Green (32025) - 1 ball
- ☐ Contrast D White (32029) - 1 ball
- ☐ Sizes U.S. K/10½ (6.5 mm) **and** U.S. N/15 (10 mm) crochet hooks **or sizes needed to obtain gauge**

STITCH GUIDE

DOUBLE-LOOP-ST

Wrap yarn around index finger twice and hold behind work, insert hook into indicated stitch and between the yarn wraps and your finger, remove your finger from wraps and draw wraps through stitch (leaving part of each wrap on other side of fabric to form loops), yarn over and draw through all loops on hook. ***Note:*** Loops form on side of fabric that is facing away from you.

INSTRUCTIONS

Note: Loopy Dots are sewn onto Blanket Base separately after Blanket Base is complete.

BLANKET BASE

With larger hook and MC, ch 106.

1st row: (RS). 1 Sc in 2nd ch from hook. *Ch 1. Skip next ch. 1 sc in next ch. Rep from * to end of chain. Turn. 105 sts.

2nd row: Ch 1. 1 sc in first sc. *1 sc in next ch-1 sp. Ch 1. Skip next sc. Rep from * to last 2 sts. 1 sc in next ch-1 sp. 1 sc in last sc. Turn.

3rd row: Ch 1. 1 sc in first sc. *Ch 1. Skip next sc. 1 sc in next ch-1 sp. Rep from * to last 2 sc. Ch 1. Skip next sc. 1 sc in last sc. Turn.

Rep last 2 rows for pat.

Cont in pat until work from beg measures 60" [152.5 cm].

Finish off.

Side edging: (RS). Join MC with sl st to bottom right corner. Ch 1. Work 1 row of sc evenly up side of Blanket. Finish off. Rep for other side.

LOOPY DOTS

(make 5 each in A, B, C, and D)

With smaller hook, ch 3.

1st rnd: 10 Double-loop-sts in 3rd ch from hook. Join with sl st to first st. 10 sts.

2nd rnd: Ch 1. 2 double-loop-sts in each st around. Join with sl st to first st. 20 sts.

3rd rnd: Ch 1. 1 double-loop-st in first st. *2 double-loop-sts in next st. 1 double-loop-st in next st. Rep from * to last st. 2 double-loop-sts in last st. Join with sl st to first st. 30 sts.

4th rnd: Ch 1. 1 double-loop-st in each of first 2 sts. *2 double-loop-sts in next st. 1 double-loop-st in each of next 2 sts. Rep from * to last st. 2 double-loop-sts in last st. Join with sl st to first st. 40 sts.

5th rnd: Ch 1. 1 double-loop-st in each of first 3 sts. *2 double-loop-sts in next st. 1 double-loop-st in each of next 3 sts. Rep from * to last st. 2 double-loop-sts in last st. Join with sl st to first st. 50 sts.

6th rnd: Ch 1. 1 double-loop-st in each of first 4 sts. *2 double-loop-sts in next st. 1 double-loop-st in each of next 4 sts. Rep from * to last st. 2 double-loop-sts in last st. Join with sl st to first st. 60 sts.

Finish off.

Beg 6" [15 cm] down from top edge and 6" [15 cm] in from side, sew Loopy Dots evenly spaced to Blanket Base as shown in diagram.

TASSELS *(make 4 with MC)*
Cut a piece of cardboard 7" [18 cm] wide. Wind yarn around cardboard 60 times. Break yarn leaving a long end and thread end through needle. Slip needle through all loops and tie tightly. Remove cardboard and wind yarn tightly around loops 2" [5 cm] below fold. Fasten securely. Cut through rem loops and trim ends evenly. Sew 1 Tassel to each corner of Blanket.

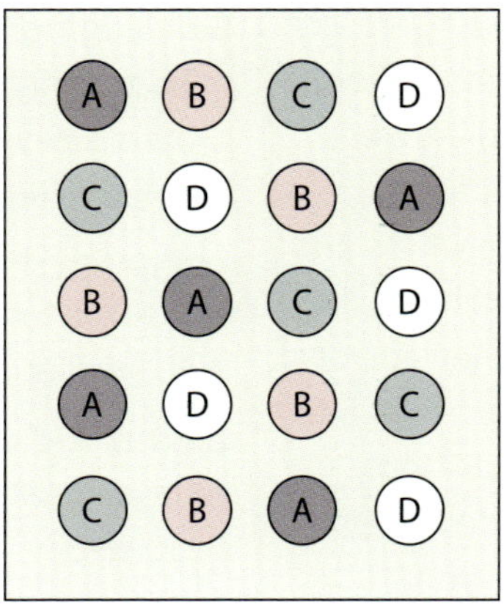

Textured Crochet Floor Pillow

EASY

MEASUREMENT
Approx 36" [91.5 cm] square

GAUGE
10 sc and 14 rows = 4" [10 cm]

MATERIALS

Bernat® Mix Home™ JUMBO 6
(8 oz/225 g; 183 yds/167 m)

- ☐ In the Clouds (97008) - 8 balls
- ☐ Size U.S. L/11 [8 mm] crochet hook **or size needed to obtain gauge**
- ☐ 20" [51 cm] diameter circular pillow form

INSTRUCTIONS

FRONT

Ch 92.

1st row: (RS). 1 Hdc in 3rd ch from hook. 1 hdc in each ch to end of chain. Turn. 90 hdc.

2nd row: Ch 2. 1 hdc in horizontal bar created below st in previous row (bar is below loops normally worked on WS—see diagram) in each hdc to end of row. Turn.

Rep 2nd row until work from beg measures 36" [91.5 cm].

Finish off.

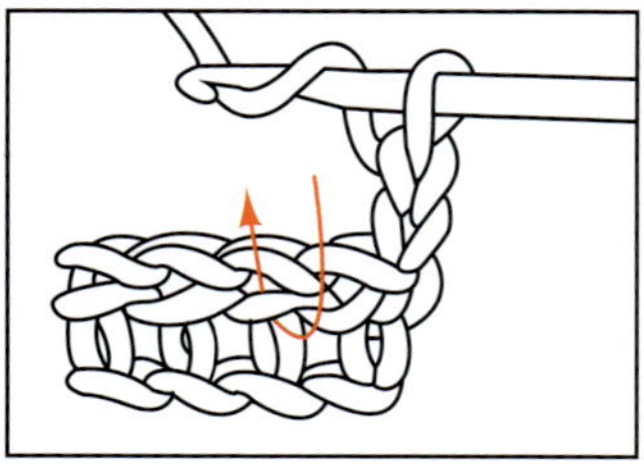

BACK *(make 2)*

Ribbing

Ch 8.

1st row: 1 Sc in 2nd ch from hook. 1 sc in each ch across. Turn. 7 sc.

2nd row: Ch 1. Working in back loops only, 1 sc in each sc to end of row. Turn.

Rep last row until work from beg (when slightly stretched) measures 36" [91.5 cm]. Do **not** fasten off.

Body

Proceed as follows:

1st row: (RS). Turn work sidewise. Ch 2. Work 90 hdc evenly across side of ribbing. Turn.

2nd row: Ch 2. 1 hdc in horizontal bar created below st in previous row (bar is below loops normally worked on WS—see diagram) in each hdc to end of row. Turn.

Rep 2nd row until work from beg measures 22" [56 cm].

Finish off.

FINISHING

Overlap Back pieces to match Front, with ribbed sections in center to create opening to insert pillow form.

Sew outer edge seams.

Tuck Stitch Knit Blanket

●●○○ **EASY**

MEASUREMENTS
Approx 43" x 55" [109 cm x 139.5 cm]

GAUGE
13 sts and 17 rows = 4" [10 cm] in stocking st

MATERIALS

Bernat® Maker Home Dec™ (BULKY 5)
(8.8 oz/250 g; 317 yds/290 m)

- ☐ Cream (11009) - 7 balls
- ☐ Size U.S. 11 (8 mm) circular knitting needle 36" [91.5 cm] long **or size needed to obtain gauge**
- ☐ Locking ring stitch markers

PATTERN STITCH

TUCK ST PANEL PAT

(worked over 17 sts)

(see Chart on page 35)

1st row: (RS). K2. P1. Place first marker on last st. K7. P1. Place second marker on last st. K6.

2nd to 6th rows: Beg on a purl row, work 5 rows in stocking st.

7th row: (RS – tuck row). K6.

Insert left-hand needle from WS through 2 vertical bars of first marked st 6 rows **below**.

K2tog (picked up 2 bars and next st).

K3. P1. Place marker on last st. K3. Insert left-hand needle from WS through 2 vertical bars of second marked st 6 rows **below**. K2tog (picked up 2 bars and next st). K2.

8th to 12th rows: Beg on a purl row, work 5 rows in stocking st.

13th row: (RS – tuck row). K2. P1. Place first marker on last st. K3. Insert right-hand needle from WS through 2 vertical bars of marked st 6 rows **below**. Slip these 2 bars onto left-hand needle. K2tog (picked up 2 bars and next st). K3. P1. Place second marker on last st. K6.

14th to 18th rows: Beg on a purl row, work 5 rows in stocking st.

Rep 7th to 18th rows for pat.

INSTRUCTIONS

BLANKET

Cast on 149 sts. Do **not** join in rnd. Working back and forth across needle in rows, proceed as follows:

1st row: (RS). *K1. P1. Rep from * to end of row.

2nd and 3rd rows: *P1. K1. Rep from * to end of row.

4th row: As 1st row.

Rep these 4 rows for Moss St pat twice **more**.

Proceed in pat as follows:

1st row: (RS). (K1. P1) 4 times. P1. *Work 1st row of Tuck St Panel Pat. P1. (P1. K1) 9 times. P2. Rep from * twice **more**. Work 1st row of Tuck St Panel Pat. P1. (P1. K1) 4 times.

2nd row: (P1. K1) 4 times. K1. *Work 2nd row of Tuck St Panel Pat. K1. (K1. P1) 9 times. K2. Rep from * twice **more**. Work 2nd row of Tuck St Panel Pat. K1. (K1. P1) 4 times.

3rd row: (P1. K1) 4 times. P1. *Work 3rd row of Tuck St Panel Pat. P1. (K1. P1) 10 times. Rep from * twice **more**. Work 3rd row of Tuck St Panel Pat. P1. (K1. P1) 4 times.

4th row: (K1. P1) 4 times. K1. *Work 4th row of Tuck St Panel Pat. K1. (P1. K1) 10 times. Rep from * twice **more**. Work 4th row of Tuck St Panel Pat. K1. (P1. K1) 4 times.

Tuck St Panel pat and Moss St pat are now in position.

Cont in pat until work from beg measures approx 58" [147.5 cm], ending on 8th or 14th row of Tuck St Panel Pat.

Work 12 rows in Moss St pat.

Bind off.

Double Wrap Tassels (make 12): Wrap yarn around a 10" [25.5 cm] piece of cardboard 30 times. Tie securely at one end. Cut across opposite end.

Wrap yarn 6 times around tassel 1½" [4 cm] from tied end and fasten securely. Wrap yarn 6 times around tassel 2¾" [7 cm] from tied end and fasten securely. Attach 6 tassels evenly spaced across top and bottom edges of Blanket.

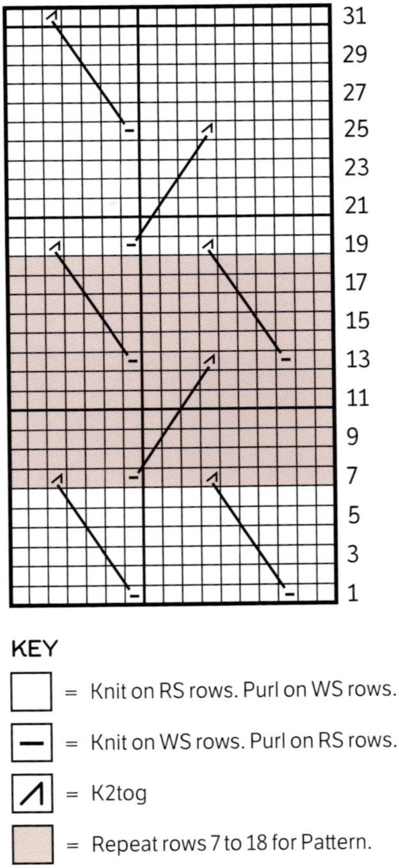

Prismatic Crochet Wall Hanging

EASY

MEASUREMENT

Approx 5" [12.5 cm] diameter, excluding fringe.

GAUGE

12 sc and 14 rows = 4" [10 cm]

MATERIALS

Caron® x Pantone™
(3.5 oz/100 g; 127 yds/116 m)

☐ Ocean Surf (01008) - 1 braid

☐ Size U.S. J/10 (6 mm) crochet hook **or size needed to obtain gauge**

☐ Five 5" [12.5 cm] brass hoops

☐ Tapestry needle

INSTRUCTIONS

Notes:

- Before working with Caron® x Pantone™ multi-shade yarn braid, separate each color link and wind into 5 separate balls.

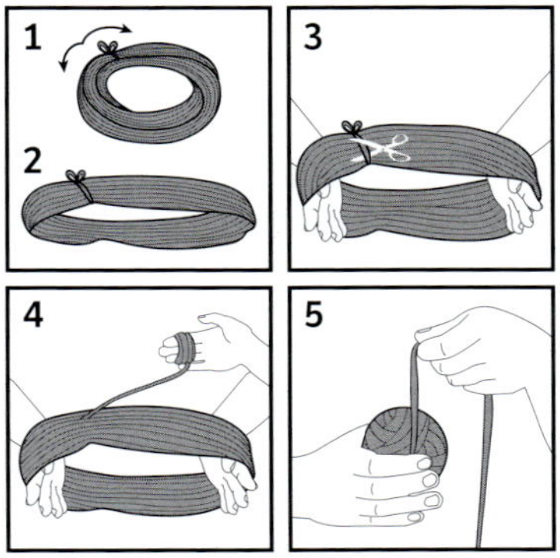

- Each color link will be referenced by its Pantone # *(see below)*.

A: 11-4001	**D:** 19-4004
B: 13-0000	**E:** 19-4026
C: 16-0000	

- Designate each different shade of the 5 separate yarn balls as Contrast A, B, C, D and E as noted in Materials section (or as desired).
- Due to finite amount of yarn in each shade, pattern gauge must be matched to ensure successful results.
- Each link will make one wall hanging.

WALL HANGING
(make 1 with each color link)

Top of Hoop

1st row: (RS). Work 16 sc in hoop. Finish off.

Bottom of Hoop

Work as for Top of Hoop.

With WS facing, pivot Top and Bottom rows of sc to inside of Hoop so RS of sts are facing *(see Weaving Diagram).*

Weaving: Cut one strand of yarn 180" [457.5 cm] long. With RS facing, secure one end of strand to right-most st at bottom **(1A in diagram).** With tapestry needle, weave strand down through left-most st at top **(1B in diagram)**, up through next st at bottom **(2A)**, down through next st at top **(2B)**, pulling strand tightly *(see diagram).* Cont in this manner until all sts have been woven into.

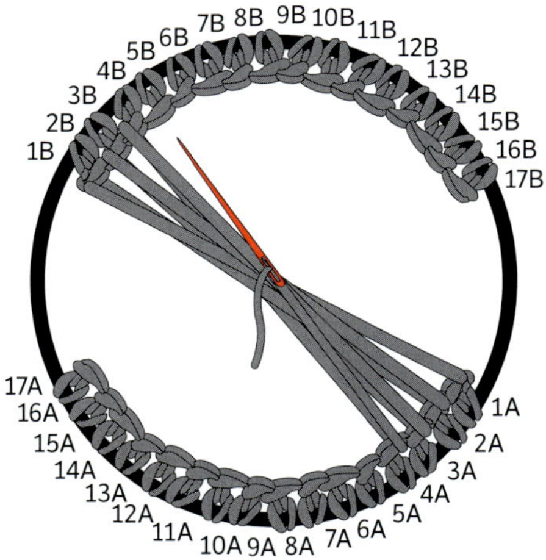

Weaving Diagram

Hanging Loop: Work 1 sc in 8th sp at Top of Hoop (sp between 8th and 9th sc). Ch 20. Sl st in first sc to form Hanging Loop. Finish off.

Fringe: Cut 15 strands of yarn each 24" [61 cm] long. Taking 1 strand, fold in half and knot into fringe in every sp between sc across Bottom of Hoop.

Trim fringe evenly.

Tufted Crochet Pillow

EASY

MEASUREMENT

Approx 20" [51 cm] diameter

GAUGE

10 sc and 11 rows = 4" [10 cm]

MATERIALS

SUPER BULKY 5

Bernat® Velvet™
(10.5 oz/300 g; 315 yds/288 m)

- ☐ Vapor Gray (32001) **or** Quiet Pink (32013) **or** White (32029) - 2 balls for **each** pillow
- ☐ Size U.S. K/10½ (6.5 mm) crochet hook **or size needed to obtain gauge**
- ☐ 20" [51 cm] diameter circular pillow form
- ☐ 2 buttons - 1" [2.5 cm]

INSTRUCTIONS

Note: Ch 2 at beg of rnd does **not** count as hdc.

FRONT and BACK *(make 2 alike)*
Ch 3.

1st rnd: 10 Hdc in 3rd ch from hook. Join with sl st to 1st hdc. 10 hdc.

2nd rnd: Ch 2. 2 hdc in each hdc around. Join with sl st to first hdc. 20 hdc.

3rd rnd: Ch 2. 1 hdc in first hdc. *2 hdc in next hdc. 1 hdc in next hdc. Rep from * to last hdc. 2 hdc in last hdc. Join with sl st to first hdc. 30 hdc.

4th rnd: Ch 2. 1 hdc in each of first 2 hdc. *2 hdc in next hdc. 1 hdc in each of next 2 hdc. Rep from * to last hdc. 2 hdc in last hdc. Join with sl st to first hdc. 40 hdc.

5th rnd: Ch 2. 1 hdc in each of first 3 hdc. *2 hdc in next hdc. 1 hdc in each of next 3 hdc. Rep from * to last hdc. 2 hdc in last hdc. Join with sl st to first hdc. 50 hdc.

6th rnd: Ch 2. 1 hdc in each of first 4 hdc. *2 hdc in next hdc. 1 hdc in each of next 4 hdc. Rep from * to last hdc. 2 hdc in last hdc. Join with sl st to first hdc. 60 hdc.

7th rnd: Ch 2. 1 hdc in each of first 5 hdc. *2 hdc in next hdc. 1 hdc in each of next 5 hdc. Rep from * to last hdc. 2 hdc in last hdc. Join with sl st to first hdc. 70 hdc.

8th rnd: Ch 2. 1 hdc in each of first 6 hdc. *2 hdc in next hdc. 1 hdc in each of next 6 hdc. Rep from * to last hdc. 2 hdc in last hdc. Join with sl st to first hdc. 80 hdc.

9th to 18th rnds: Cont in this manner, inc 10 hdc evenly around each rnd until there are 180 hdc.

Do **not** finish off.

Join Front and Back: With WS of Front and Back tog, ch 1. Working through **both** thicknesses, work 1 sc in each st around, insert pillow form at halfway point and cont around to end. Join with sl st to first sc. Finish off.

BUTTON COVER

Ch 3.

1st rnd: 10 Hdc in 3rd ch from hook. Join with sl st to first hdc.

2nd rnd: Ch 2. 1 hdc in each st around. Join with sl st to first hdc. Insert button.

Finish off, leaving a long end. Draw end through rem sts and fasten securely around button.

Rep for 2nd button.

General Instructions

ABBREVIATIONS

Approx	Approximately
beg	beginning
ch	chain(s)
cont	continue
cm	centimeters
dc	double crochet(s)
Dc3(5)tog	double crochet 3(5) together
g	grams
hdc	half double crochet(s)
inc	increase
K	knit
m	meters
mm	millimeters
MC	Main Color
oz	ounces
P	purl
Pat	Pattern
rem	remain(ing)
rep	repeat
Rnd(s)	Round(s)
RS	right side
sc	single crochet(s)
Sc2tog	single crochet 2 together
Sl1P	Slip next stitch purlwise
sl st	slip stitch
sp(s)	space(s)
st(s)	stitch(es)
tog	together
WS	wrong side
yds	yards
Yoh	Yarn over hook

KNIT TERMINOLOGY

UNITED STATES		INTERNATIONAL
gauge	=	tension
bind off	=	cast off
yarn over (YO)	=	yarn forward (yfwd) **or** yarn around needle (yrn)

CROCHET TERMINOLOGY

UNITED STATES		INTERNATIONAL
slip stitch (slip st)	=	single crochet (sc)
single crochet (sc)	=	double crochet (dc)
half double crochet (hdc)	=	half treble crochet (htr)
double crochet (dc)	=	treble crochet (tr)
treble crochet (tr)	=	double treble crochet (dtr)
double treble crochet (dtr)	=	triple treble crochet (ttr)
triple treble crochet (tr tr)	=	quadruple treble crochet (qtr)
skip	=	miss

KNITTING NEEDLES

UNITED STATES	ENGLISH U.K.	METRIC (mm)
0	13	2
1	12	2.25
2	11	2.75
3	10	3.25
4	9	3.5
5	8	3.75
6	7	4
7	6	4.5
8	5	5
9	4	5.5
10	3	6
10½	2	6.5
11	1	8
13	00	9
15	000	10
17	---	12.75
19	---	15
35	---	19
50	---	25

CROCHET HOOKS

U.S.	Metric mm
B-1	2.25
C-2	2.75
D-3	3.25
E-4	3.5
F-5	3.75
G-6	4
7	4.5
H-8	5
I-9	5.5
J-10	6
K-10½	6.5
L-11	8
M/N-13	9
N/P-15	10
P/Q	15
Q	16
S	19

BASIC	Projects using basic stitches. May include basic increases and decreases.
EASY	Projects may include simple stitch patterns, color work, and/or shaping.
INTERMEDIATE	Projects may include involved stitch patterns, color work, and/or shaping.
COMPLEX	Projects may include complex stitch patterns, color work, and/or shaping using a variety of techniques and stitches simultaneously.

Yarn Weight Symbol & Names	LACE 0	SUPER FINE 1	FINE 2	LIGHT 3	MEDIUM 4	BULKY 5	SUPER BULKY 6	JUMBO 7
Type of Yarns in Category	Fingering, size 10 crochet thread	Sock, Fingering, Baby	Sport, Baby	DK, Light Worsted	Worsted, Afghan, Aran	Chunky, Craft, Rug	Super Bulky, Roving	Jumbo, Roving
Knit Gauge Ranges in Stockinette St to 4" (10 cm)	33-40 sts**	27-32 sts	23-26 sts	21-24 sts	16-20 sts	12-15 sts	7-11 sts	6 sts and fewer
Advised Needle Size Range	000 to 1	1 to 3	3 to 5	5 to 7	7 to 9	9 to11	11 to 17	17 and larger

* GUIDELINES ONLY: The chart above reflects the most commonly used gauges and needle sizes for specific yarn categories.

** Lace weight yarns are usually knitted on larger needles to create lacy openwork patterns. Accordingly, a gauge range is difficult to determine. Always follow the gauge stated in your pattern.

Yarn Weight Symbol & Names	LACE 0	SUPER FINE 1	FINE 2	LIGHT 3	MEDIUM 4	BULKY 5	SUPER BULKY 6	JUMBO 7
Type of Yarns in Category	Fingering, size 10 crochet thread	Sock, Fingering, Baby	Sport, Baby	DK, Light Worsted	Worsted, Afghan, Aran	Chunky, Craft, Rug	Super Bulky, Roving	Jumbo, Roving
Crochet Gauge* Ranges in Single Crochet to 4" (10 cm)	32-42 sts**	21-32 sts	16-20 sts	12-17 sts	11-14 sts	8-11 sts	6-9 sts	5 sts and fewer
Advised Hook Size Range	Steel*** 6 to 8, Regular hook B-1	B-1 to E-4	E-4 to 7	7 to I-9	I-9 to K-10½	K-10½ to M/N-13	M/N-13 to Q	Q and larger

*GUIDELINES ONLY: The chart above reflects the most commonly used gauges and hook sizes for specific yarn categories.

** Lace weight yarns are usually crocheted with larger hooks to create lacy openwork patterns. Accordingly, a gauge range is difficult to determine. Always follow the gauge stated in your pattern.

*** Steel crochet hooks are sized differently from regular hooks–the higher the number, the smaller the hook, which is the reverse of regular hook sizing.

SYMBOLS & TERMS

* — work instructions following * as many more times as indicated in addition to the first time.

( ) or [ ] — work enclosed instructions as many times as specified by the number immediately following or work all enclosed instructions in the stitch or space indicated or contains explanatory remarks.

GAUGE

Exact gauge is essential for proper size or fit. Before beginning your project, make a sample swatch in the yarn and hookorneedlesspecified. After completing your swatch, measure it, counting your stitches and rows carefully. If your swatch is larger or smaller than specified, **make another, changing hook or needle size to get the correct gauge**. Keep trying until you find the size hook or needles that will give you the specified gauge. Once proper gauge is obtained, measure widthe of piece approximately every 3" [7.5 cm] to be sure gauge remains consistent.

ZEROS

To consolidate the length of an involved pattern, zeros are sometimes used so that all sizes can be combined. For example, K0 (0-11) means the largest size would knit 11 and the first two sizes would do nothing.

BACK OR FRONT LOOP ONLY

Work only in loop(s) indicated by arrow ***(Fig. 1)***.

Fig. 1

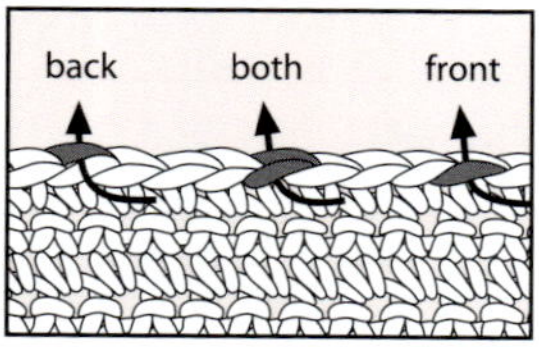

FREE LOOPS

After working in Back or Front Loops Only on a row or round, there will be a ridge of unused loops. These are called the free loop. Later, when instructed to work in the free loops of the same row or round, work in these loops ***(Fig. 2a)***.

When instructed to work in free loops of a chain, work in loop indicated by arrow ***(Fig. 2b)***.

Fig. 2a

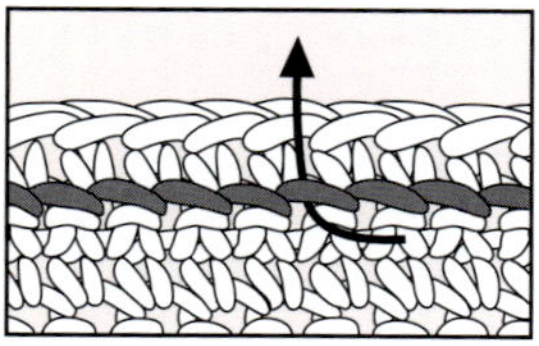

Fig. 2b

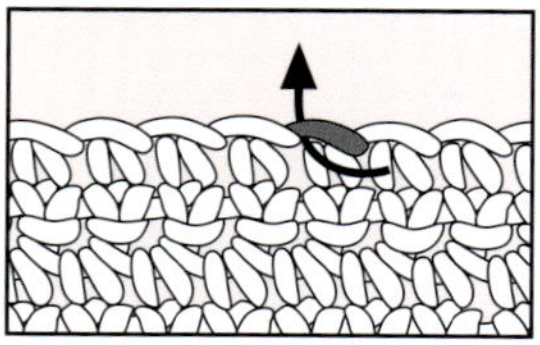

REVERSE SINGLE CROCHET

Working from **left** to **right**, * insert hook in stitch to right of hook ***(Fig. 3a)***, Yoh and draw through, under and to left of loop on hook (2 loops on hook) ***(Fig. 3b)***, Yoh and draw through both loops on hook ***(Fig. 3c)*** **(reverse sc made,** ***Fig. 3d*****)**; repeat from * around.

Fig. 3a

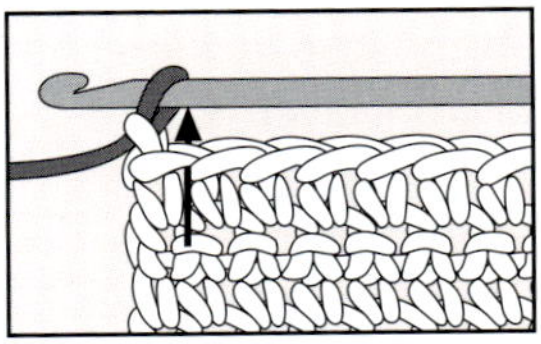

Fig. 3b

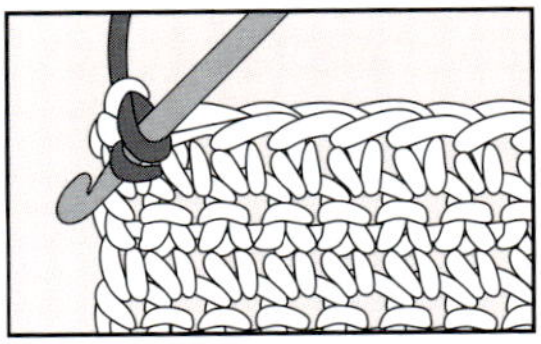

Fig. 3c

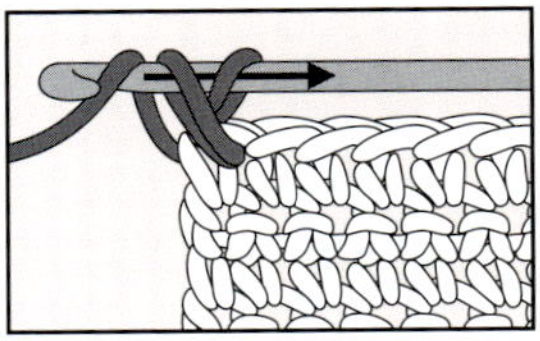

Fig. 3d

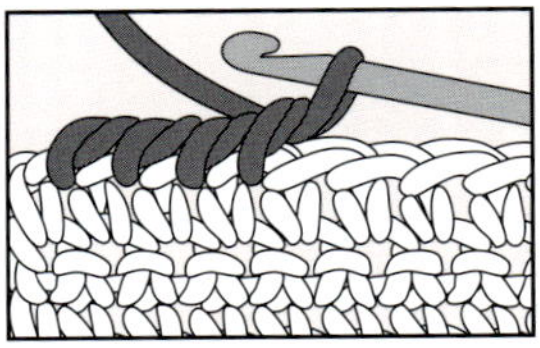

FRINGE

Cut a piece of cardboard 6" [15 cm] wide and half as long as specified in individual instructions for strands. Wind the yarn **loosely** and **evenly** around the cardboard lenthwise until the card is filled, then cut across one end; repeat as needed.

Hold together as many strands as specified in individual instructions; fold in half.

With **wrong** side facing and using a crochet hook, draw the folded end up through a stitch or space and pull the loose ends through the folded end ***(Fig. 4a & c)***; draw the knot up **tightly** ***(Fig. 4b & d)***. Repeat, spacing as specified in individual instructions.

Lay flat on a hard surface and trim the ends.

Fig. 4a

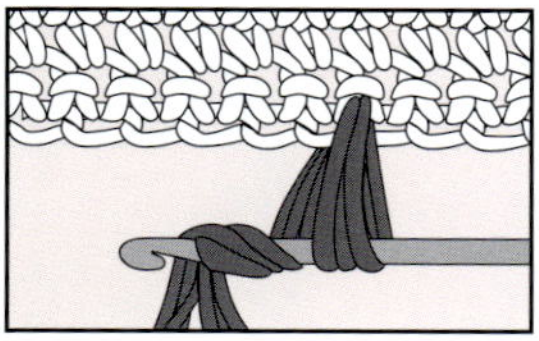

Fig. 4b

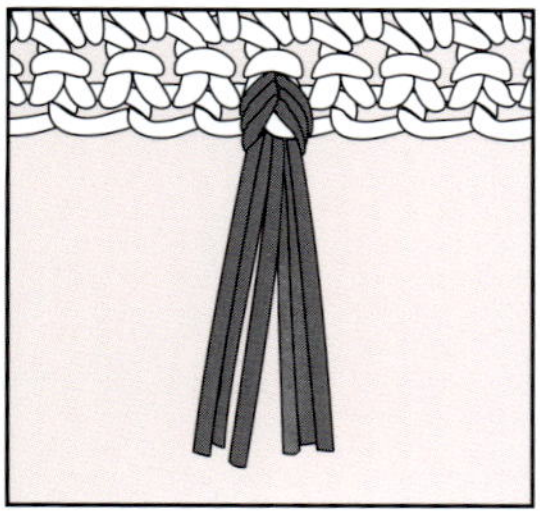

Fig. 4c

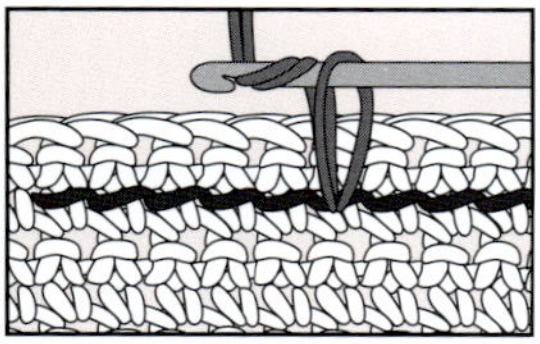

Fig. 4d

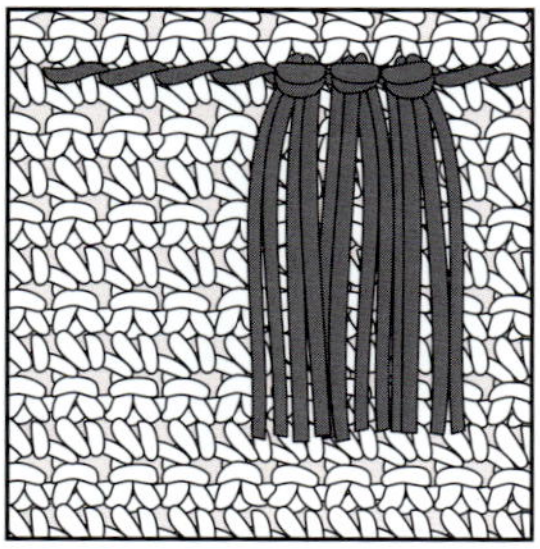

TASSEL

Cut a piece of cardboard as long as specified in individual instructions. Wind the yarn around the cardboard as many times as indicated in individual instructions. Cut an 18" [45.5 cm] length of yarn and insert it under all of the strands at the top of the cardboard; pull up **tightly** and tie securely. Leave the yarn ends long enough to attach the tassel. Cut the yarn at the opposite end of the cardboard and then remove it ***(Fig. 5a)***. Cut a length of yarn and wrap it tightly around the tassel as indicated in individual instructions ***(Fig. 5b)***; tie securely. Trim the ends.

Fig. 5a

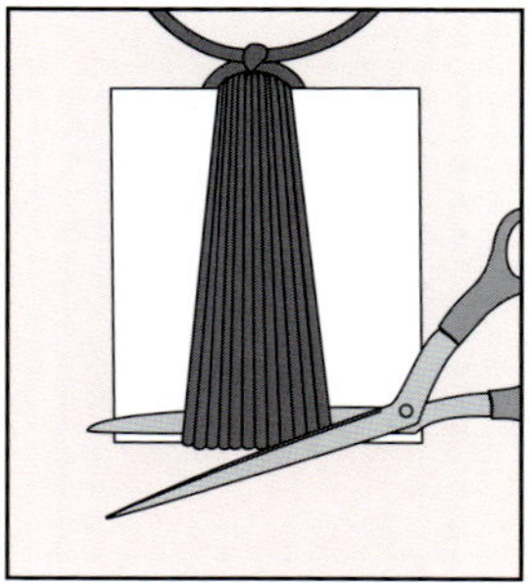

Fig. 5b

Made In U.S.A.

We have made every effort to ensure that these instructions are accurate and complete. We cannot, however, be responsible for human error, typographica mistakes, or variations in individual work.